Lamenting While Doing
Laps in the Lake

Poems

by

Bill Ratner

ISBN: 9798338782460
Printed in the United States of America
First Edition

Copyright©2024: Bill Ratner
Published by Slow Lightning Lit

Editor-in-Chief, Design
Peggy Dobreer, Slow Lightning Lit

Book Format, Interior Consultant
Shannon Therese, Picture Show Press

Website, Technical Assistance
Tiago Augusto Souza Barreiro

Author Photo
John Exley

Cover Comments
Donna Baier-Stein
Terry Wolverton

Introduction
Art Hanlon

Published by Slow Lightning Lit

www. slowlightninglit.com
Printed in the United States of America

This book of poems is dedicated

⌒

To those who went before:
my beloved mother, father,
and my brother Pete.

⌒

And to those who came after:
my wife & kids,
my aunts and uncles, my stepmother,
camp counsellors, teachers, editors, shrinks,
and soda jerks.

Yet this I call to mind and therefore have hope...

—Lamentations 3:21

INTRODUCTION

I remember the day Bill Ratner put me in touch with gravity. We were on our way to a favorite Mexican restaurant when he casually detoured down Baxter Street, one of the steepest streets in Los Angeles. Gravity had me hanging from my seat belt as if from a parachute harness in the cockpit of a dive bomber. I felt as if we were falling rather than driving down an unforgiving hill while Bill softly laughed—not at my discomfort, but at my astonished surprise that Los Angeles even had such a hill—much less a hill with a 32% grade. The roadway seemed paved with rubble, and parked cars made for a narrow corridor. For an endless, few seconds everything hung in the balance. Will the brakes hold? What happens if we meet another car coming up from below? Suppose we have what insurance companies call Acts of God? Earthquake? Fire? Our tour had turned into a most intriguing and unexpectedly focused ride. This was Bill's attempt to show me a Los Angeles that exists outside the glare of mythic Hollywood land.

And so it is with Lamenting While Doing Laps in the Lake, this book of poems in your hand—utterly serious, subtly hopeful, delightfully amusing, humanely and hysterically funny, and yet the subject of an intense meditation that tries to understand and cope with the inexplicable fact of suffering. Lamenting While Doing Laps in the Lake contains poems that explore the possibility of finding a moral compass to guide us through an unrelenting and unforgiving life of travail. Every poem in this collection represents a concentrated moment when everything hangs in the balance. What does it take, this beautiful collection of poems asks, to tip the equation?

Lamenting While Doing Laps in the Lake is a radical work of art that defies self-pity, regales life's miniscule delights in big ways, and does so through every trial without ever evoking anger or succumbing to despair—a stellar accomplishment. Read on.

Art Hanlon,
Associate Poetry Editor,
Narrative Magazine

TABLE OF CONTENTS

I.   Youth

II.   Age

I.   Youth

Family Forensics

I made dioramas as a child
mystery houses
knife nicks in a door frame
whispers in the hallway
night lights
a pre-dawn blue
to keep nightmares away
I used bendy dolls
tiny people
like pipe cleaners
a head bends, a leg twists
you lay them down
in any position
from endearment
to death by strangulation
bendy children
you could imagine as happy
with toys, balls, and sticks
but grandparents found dead
mothers tied up
babies shrieking
like drunks gone dry
turn the tiny lights on
nothing changes

Delores

You ever play naked? she asked
hair smelling of Spider Lake and pinecones
I five-and-a-half, Delores seven, her eyes a feral grey.

Take down your pants, she said. *Let's smell butts.*
Thrumming like a country wind
I pulled them down.

Bend over, she said.
I turned toward the dark forest
every inch of skin a hayride.

Her nose brushed my bottom.
Your turn, she said unveiling herself.
She smelled of silt and chalk and flesh.

If you put that in this
I'll have a baby, she said.
Grownup voices wafted up the path.

We yanked our pants up and ran back down
the hill to the resort. I wanted more.
I wanted to inhale her coarse, sun-tangled hair.

Nights I writhed on mountains of imaginary Delores
mornings we flew like cherubs to the waterfront
dashed across the dock, and splashed down in Spider Lake.

At the sandy bottom we peeled aside our
swimsuits and pissed a shimmering trombone yellow.
One morning after cherry-topped pancakes I whispered,

There's no one in my room.
Tented by lilacs we strolled to my cabin
where we lay, the smell of breakfast in our hair.

The cabin door opened
my brother zombied into view
seeing what he saw—*I'M TELLING MOM!*

Next day I awoke to my mother: *I know you and Delores
are friends* (my dear mother just and fair.)
But I'd like you to play with the other children.

Later my brother's chums took me
for a ride out on Spider Lake in a dinghy.
They dropped anchor and stalled in the calm.

Tell us about Delores, they leered,
Or we'll swamp and you'll drown.
I told them. Everything.

I never saw Delores again.
Down the years, every so often
at school, the mall, the most innocent of places

a teenage boy approaches
and whispers in my ear
Tell me, how's Delores?

"That Your Heart Longs For"

—a lingerie marketing slogan

I clipped stacks of brassiere and panty ads
  from the society pages—
    Maidenform Caprice Perma-Lift
     faces tilted back gazing up.

This one would be nice to me...
 not this one no she wouldn't care
  I can tell. This one maybe
   a soft look to her eyes.

Huntresses
 in organza silk
  find me injured
   carry me to a clearing.

Miss Wisconsin shiny black pumps pleated white swimsuit
 hands resting on her sumptuous hips
  her dark hair and soft breasts
   reminding me of my mother—

Her mastectomy scar.
 My stepmother found my collection
  in my toy UPS semi-truck
   (no one knew that corner of my closet.)

   I found your pictures.
    I've decided not to tell your father.

Devotions of the Ordinary

At sleep-away camp
  I pee next to this blonde boy
    into a rusted enamel trough.

He stares at the circumcision scar on my penis.
  What happened? he says like he's witnessed
  a bike accident. *The doctor did that,* I say.

God did that, he says, revealing an inculcation
  at the hands of an older brother
    or Sunday school teacher.

God isn't everywhere at camp.
  What is important is being friends.

Counselors tell ghost stories, fables, trickster tales.
  At night we recite: *Yea, though I walk through the*
    valley of the shadow of death I will fear no evil.

I keep seeing this bucolic Swiss valley
  where cows bathe in spring water
    and danger lurks behind rocks.

I'm walking through the valley alone
    and I do fear evil.

Crawl Space

In the bottom drawer of my bedstand
I kept a Christmas candle—a choirboy
holding a hymnal, mouth open in song,
wick protruding from his head.
I lit him on fire.

A pair of loose boards lay end-to-end
in my closet crammed with Lincoln Logs,
comic books, a UPS truck stuffed
with brassiere and pantie ads from
The Family Section of the Star-Tribune.

Careful to avoid splinters I dragged myself
along the wooden planks
under our steep mansard roof.
The windowless space smelled
of pine and creosote.

Dried plaster oozed from between strips of lath
in shapes of ogres and gnomes.
The melting choirboy's face dripped
down his vestments into cracks in the wood floor
igniting like a tiny sea at war.

Where are you?
came the muffled voice of my mother.
I swatted out the flames,
fingers coated in hot wax.

The darkness absorbed
the sounds of my breathing.
She tapped her foot on the carpeted floor.
I lay on the other side of the wall.

Driving Under

I never knew my father as a death man
He could kill us, my brother said.
I was mystified by the gulf between them
sailor blood, family blood.

The Navy gave my father a hand-painted nameplate
that sits by a muddy canteen
he took off a corpse of a Japanese soldier.
J.E. Ratner, Executive Officer - Fancy. War.

My brother arrived on the Camp White Earth bus
backslapping his friends. He ignored me.
That, and our mom was dead.

My counsellor Jerry had us eight-year-olds do laps
in the lake. Camouflaged by spring-fed waves
I searched for the ghosts Jerry told us about
after lights out.

I rolled toward the sandy bottom and let out a good cry
as my mother used to call it, like knowing how to pee
without dripping on your pants, holding your fork right,
Tears can pass for lake water.

First One Free

Late one night playing cowboys and war
John Waterhouse and I
placed pillows on the rug
dropped to our knees huffed and puffed deep and fast

crammed our thumbs in our mouths
blew hard like into weather balloons
passed out

and came to
face down in a pillow
stoned like our fathers

Breaking Wind

My first brush with God I pumped my trike fast
up the driveway, stomach gas filling me
I tried to hold it.
My older brother shouted *Stop breaking wind!*
I apologized to God *I am sorry for breaking wind.*

I've always wondered how that slippage
sparked my guilt the mystery
like the verse in John:
The wind bloweth where it listeth,
and thou hearest the sound thereof...

Next time I talked to God
I prayed for my brother's health
I didn't learn this at church or the dinner table
we didn't pray though we were churchgoers
Ben Franklin-style Unitarians worshippers of Nature God

God in garlic plants loamy dirt walnut trees.
I prayed not feeling a deeply embedded faith
that anyone or anything was listening
a pro forma sort of prayer
necessary to do.

Months drew on, my brother's health dwindled
I continued to pray. After he died
I think I issued one last prayer:
Thanks for nothing.
Thanks for less than nothing.

Duck and Cover

Ack-ack-ack—40-millimeter machine guns
ratchet the nose of a Russian Mig
six-year-olds dodge through recess
enemy planes vie for A-bomb time
victory or red death
heaven or magma
blood or evaporation—
Duck and Cover
black & white school film stars the man
with the voice—*Duck and Cover*
crawl under your desk we're in this together—
Duck and Cover
earth Christmasy and green
now charred bare—
Duck and Cover
evil fairytale beings
hide along the dreary way
fly up out of the thorny bush
shave our heads take our gold
bird-shaped shadows cross the horizon
carrying the next world

They Send Me to the City to Stay with My Auntie

I hang my jacket in the hallway
her apartment is old
made from shoestring potatoes
smells like a jelly factory.

Against the wall a man's face
eyes folded
laces around his neck
That's your uncle, dear.

He barred her
from doing much of anything
when he was around
then he died.

She asked the doctors
to keep his eyes and brain
alive and put them
in a fish tank.

That night when she got home
she put on a mambo record
poured herself a vodka lit a cigarette
and blew smoke in his eyes.

The tank is down the hall
full of algae and bubbles
she has it hidden
behind a curtain.

On the wall are photos
of President Gerald Ford
our family on vacation
and antique pictures of naked ladies.

How many naked ladies do I watch
before I get a chocolate sundae? I ask.

I'll think about it, she says.
Behind the curtain skirts are hung up
sponges tied together
a bag of teeth.

My Auntie takes a photo of me
so my parents will see
the child they raised
buzz-cut roadworthy.

My Auntie tells me stories
about my family
takes me shopping
for sweaters and penny loafers.

When she gets excited
she makes the sound
of a happy seagull
and spins like a mooring buoy.

Small Voice

In the south transept of Basilica of St. Mary
confessionals are lined up like Porta-Johns
priests suggest *Hail Marys Our Fathers* doors creak
confessors unfold and tiptoe back to the sanctuary.

Go, my friend Pat says.

What do I say? I whisper, *I've never been to confession.*

Tell him you want to be Catholic.

I sit on the tiny wooden bench
a woven rattan screen like on my grandma's dining room chair
separates me from the priest
a tan shadow breathing.

What is your confession?

He sounds like the announcer on Channel Seven.

I take a breath, *I'm half-Jewish*
I go to the Unitarian Church I want to be Catholic.

He rises, his body tall
and blurry through the screen.

His shoes scrape the floor.
In a deep monotone he says,

Pray for faith.

My Father Sings

Bird noises while we shop at Mall of America—
labyrinthine architectonic cathedrals lined up for
miles one store after another. *Owk-owk-owk!* He
sounds like a Muscovy duck emerging from its nest,
hunting insects to eat. It embarrasses me, but I am
proud of his big, hairy chest, his five-fingered
outfielder's mitt, an oversized leather work glove that
was supposed to save the bones in his hand from
shattering at a line drive. His cries bounce off the
stucco walls. Passersby stare up as if the noise is
coming from the mall's high ceilings. His cries slap
against jewelry stores, sport shoe stores, employee-
only spaces. *Owk-owk-owk!* I laugh the way you'd laugh
at a kayaker waving his arms as he slides over the
edge of Niagara. My dad likes it when I laugh. He also
makes noises when he takes a shower, but quieter,
often in Yiddish. He clucks at the end of the chorus.
Lomir alle singen, nack, nack, nack, as if to irritate his
own father.

To Shoot a Gun

Businessmen invited my father to go deer hunting
he didn't know forests growing up behind a cigar store.

What the hell do I want to shoot a deer for?
I liked this streak of peace in him.

At Camp White Earth I took to the rifle range
.22-caliber one-shot rifles warm polished walnut

butt of the gun pressed against my cheek
long-rifle bullets smelled like firecrackers after the bang

paper targets count your score by the round rips
no human face no eyeless man silhouettes

circles within circles white to black
what a soft lead projectile would do to a face, a foot.

Our counselor Jerry told us some kid
blasted his big toe off—spatter of child blood

like a movie special effect; we all laughed
but the spatter stayed with me.

Learned at camp:
a good aim,
blast the wilderness,
shooting is math in the air.

my brother is a dark circus

there are no tickets
no calliope no cotton candy
the master of ceremonies a quiet horse
my brother broken clay

his breath a vault the nurses can't fill
they love him
the smell of his skin
at its shelf life

my mother in the bleachers
curled around her cigarette
aging in starched summer cottons
a tragic wisdom

my father a ten-pound hammer
cables loose
the moon
through a tear in the roof

my brother on a roped platform
over a tiny pool below
swim now
like when you were Captain.

you leave the ring
angry at your limitations
needles laundry bags
no longer needed

girls bring picnics
and cry
did you date them all
you are the doom they know

clowns and roughnecks sit stone-still
the tent is blind
we mourn
your finished spirit

Tough Love Summer

A large creature, as tall as a tree,
with a lipless mouth and jagged teeth.
Its breath was a strange hiss,
its footprints full of blood.
—Ojibwa Legend

Fake wolf cries tear through the silence
our camp counsellor pounds the outside walls of our cabin

howling like he's going to vomit
pretending he's a creature named Wendigo

Native American serial killer
who specializes in eating young campers.

A few boys burst into tears
I know this game I've got an older brother.

In the morning a boy plays
reveille on a coronet as we salute.

The rope and pulley clank against the flag pole
like ghosts in a haunted mansion

The food is good, we pour fistfuls of sugar
on waffles burned just right.

She Took the Car

My babysitter Susie drove us to Powderhorn Park
in my dad's car and hooked up with guys
in greasy t-shirts. Mine was clean and ironed.
Her boys talked in farm tones
wore new man beards and rolled up cuffs.

One had a gun. I saw it like you spot a jackrabbit
frozen, then gone.
Her pal Robby got shot in the bicep,
bled like he shouldered a thorn bush.
The shooter faded away.

The cops were coming.
This wouldn't have happened at Lynnhurst Field
where green-eyed kids played
in Lutheran jerseys, lutefisk and fish soup
waiting for them back at the house.

My dad's Packard sedan was clean
with a proper garage to come home to.
Susie's boys crammed in the back shouting stuff
that can put you in the path of a gun
like the Purple Gang movie.

They said it was a .22. I shot a .22 at camp,
bullets smaller than Sweetarts, enough to rip through
Robby's Minnesota skin spurting blood
on my dad's backseat. They didn't know where to go
scared the hospital would report the wound.

Susie was a bigger boss
than any of them.
She kicked those boys out of the car.
We tore off through half-hearted shouts.
I listened for the echo of gunfire.

Empathy

I do this thing lately
with how I see a person.

I imagine what I'd find
if I peeled back their face.

Behind their mouth,
behind their eyes—

bone
gristle
fear
need
the ability to love.

They are not the enemy.

In Adolescence Moods Pass Like Hearses

Strangers show up for my father's funeral
women in pressed cotton
men with clipped Van Dykes
all smelling of cake and chips.

Swallows pitch and yaw in tight swirls
making my dog look up.
My father's voice was fast and rich
like his shoeshines like chocolate sauce.

The week of his funeral the Boulevard Matinee
shows *Swiss Family Robinson*, President Kennedy
promotes bomb shelters, the popular boys at school meet up
at Minnehaha Creek with .22-caliber rifles and fire at each other.

I sit at the curb and write in my journal. A police car drives up.
The boys stop shooting. *What are you doing?*
the officer asks me, neck spilling over his blue wool collar,
Writing a ghost story?

My father's casket is heavy
giving the impression
he isn't ready to leave.

Prancing

Like Nureyev only sassy
legs a blur of moves
eyes like a discus thrower
dead brother Pete joins me
he's slower taller
like Gregory Hines without the smile
dad steps in fast
head up chest out legs spinning
like helicopter seeds
mom's gone
just us now
who is watching
try on a face
The Dancer
The Orphan
The Mourner

True North

On the wall a framed photo of my family—
my father in shorts that show his knees
the gurgle of authority in his voice.

Holding a salad, my mother, small in an oval hat
shaped like a nun's headgear makes me wonder
if she was preoccupied with evil.

I, a tiny lad, tight in my cottons, sit on lawn furniture.
How many tired, woolen asses straddled those chairs?
My dog tests the air with his tongue.

On my father's desk his prized *Book of Hours*
deckled edge closed by pounded iron buckles
pages decorated with vines and wilting leaves
inked into the vellum.

Pasted on a wing of gold cloth
the epigraph: *The Byble*
Whych Is All the Holy Scripture.
My father may have suffered more than he let on.

His smelly tobacco pipes lie on the desk,
hand-drawn portolan atlases, sea charts,
an oval world map with cherubs
blowing currents of wind at the continents.

He advised me to create my own book
to stave off crime, plague, war.
He suggested that I imagine the making of the book,
the slap of metal as the inker arranges the moveable type.

I drew fences, alleys, lengths of razor wire,
and a copper compass that points true north.

II.   Age

Full Wolf Moon

Driving down Toro Canyon Road I don't turn
on the radio and erase the day.
Instead, I calculate whom I might conjure up—
my short-lived sister who would have been my guardian
the bogeymen who gather outside my house at night
dream figures in casual cottons who plan to kill me.

The moon January 25th—full wolf moon.
Clouds part like sheer curtains, big moon, silver white.
Wolves will likely howl.
I howl.
Tears feel good, an aquifer of them
blasting up like a geyser on the freeway.
Behind tinted windows no one can see.

I never knew my dead sister's name. I like Phoebe.
I howl for Phoebe, thank her for flying by one time
past my mobile home, tiny cape fluttering like Super Mouse, miniature
goddess on her rounds.
My howls shake my insides like a carnival ride.

I thank my grandson Sage for being.
I call out for my brother
his handsome photos—young, alive, green-eyed.
I bounce on my father's belly,
hug his neck and howl some more.
And my mother, how long I remember,
beautiful, struck down in innocence and sadness.

Where's the moon, Boppa, my grandson asks
at the park as the sun goes down
Where's the moony moon?

Crossfade

I spend my night like a priest
in a rental church
searching for my opening line
the purple offstage glow of the blacklight
invisible to all but us
players all in place on a thrust stage
like vanilla nut creams in a gift box
we stand in darkness breathing.
Someone whispers an acting note.
The recipient hisses like a snow goose.
A suspension harness dangles against the wall
from a past Peter Pan. I finger my props:
drill bits, wood screws, things to suggest
my character is searching for something—
the playwright's idea.
He has stopped showing up.
The lighting man rehearses a crossfade
a floodlight grows too hot like a corpse flower
smells like desiccation.
the light bar bursts its chain
and yanks the laser lights
to a flash of carnival madness.
Offstage I shout my opening line:
Wake up. Stop dreaming.
A parishioner rushes in from the street and shouts
You're doing Satan's work!
The stage manager calls
Blackout.

Bacchus in the Galleria

Tall Dionysus slides down
off the roof like Santa Claus
with a mild inebriated smile.
He speaks to me, *You're doing just fine.*
No one has ever told me such a thing
oh, my father drove up once in a dream
to tell me he was proud of me
that was nice.
My brother appeared after his death
the thin gray lid of his coffin loose
eyes open, impatient, hooded in darkness,
angry with me.

I'm not a celebrant of rapture
not much of a wine drinker
though I am in therapy the ecstasy of tears.
I take what he said as a point of pride.
Dionysus—a glaucus green moony face,
beardless with bangs like my Aunt Ann's
genuine human hair wig.
He fondles a black ribbon
cradles a crystal saucer of blood-red wine
wears fawnskin barely covering parts
his devotees pine for.

Bacchanals angered the Romans—
men and women with men and women
slaves and the young.
The Roman Senate banned his worship
perhaps because he is Greek.
Dionysus is a demigod.
Who else should I listen to?

The Ephemeral West

You come across an icon
    a jar of wonders in a museum
        light comes through a door.

A figure of fog emerges from a stone reliquary
    the shape of a coffin
        covered in garish white mold.
          Its wet hairs glisten.

I don't want a guru
   no strong man over me
     no orange robes or talk of dharma.
      The truth is in the newspaper.

I have less hair than my father.
    Am I therefore evolved?

In the darkened gallery
    it hovers like a naked root
      wings lacquered by time
        skin a polished opera stage.

It dances like a wolf
    hurtling through the flushing green
      Boddhisatva in a skin of onyx
        the Buddha of the future.

I stand before it with the formality
    of a royal wedding
      holding thoughts
        of good meals, car rides
          sandstone lions by the library.

    It wants to hold me here.
I scoot over the grass toward home

untouched by ground
    cloth-covered volumes of myth
        stacked neatly by my bed
           like children's books.

How You Find the Divine

Remember playing fish, slapping the table
   shouting *Go fish!* gathering up cards
      like power flags, like they say
you hold all the cards.

These days you sit alone pulling cards—
The Child   The Mother   The Shadow

        The Accidental One
candle flickering, no plot in the traditional sense.

Holding flowers in your head
     a mandala a manhole cover
        a coast live oak your new friend—

vague cartoons planted like beach umbrellas
   perfume the air with mildew
      from the last time you were free.

You weep for the dying mother
   gamble on the tardy child
      both sides of the coin at once
        a dawning.

My Job as an Advertising Writer Isn't What I'd Hoped

We haul, we sit
when the boss isn't looking I design
packaging with images of the young, the hairless

one hand on a balustrade
imprints of underthings on their skin
how the flesh falls when placed upside down.

We market foods named phonak, nexlon
two-syllable language eliciting optimism
belief in solutions the feeling of family.

I utilize my father's graveyard of ad words
designed to compel us to buy
Toddler Snack Solid White

Delicious for Walking
Outshined by a Dryer.
I portray children pushing at water

models with one eye
photograph a product on an outcropping
shaped like a Brahma chicken.

On the package in fine print
Do Not Feed Lightly
Do Not Confuse Food for Thought.

The Elusiveness of What We Seek

A rickety bi-plane writes messages for beachgoers:
Buy beer.
Denise will you marry me?
Vote for a candidate who loves guns.

For the moment the sky is free of accidents.
For now our problems are contained in casks
under the sea. Overcast skies tomorrow.

We've stopped asking why bullets
tearing into flesh satisfy rage.
It makes us think of burdens instead of murder.

An entire village topples down a flooded ridge
the citizenry prays to avoid the boulders.
I ask an old friend what he likes

about being an Evangelical.
He says, rubbing his eyes,
I like the rules.

Things at Work that Pass for Art

We file into the conference room—a glass whale
within a teak veneer whale—hoping for blood sugar
numbers promised on the Winchell's Donut box.
Calcified raindrops on the windows make us think it's
spring and not January when icicles turn to javelins.
The streets below are as walkable as a slip'n'slide at a
career milestone party. It's sub-zero, but in here it's
spa weather. The plasma TV is paused on news crawl:
Japan Firm Opens Whale Meat Vending Machines. The
Paste-up Team slides film onto the overhead
projector—a cat food box/ a six-pack/ a lip balm
label. Digital brainstorming filters our blood like a
liver in recovery. Smiling Buddha with steel balls in
his hand rests above a stack of never-opened cartons
that quiver with the building. Red balloons *STOP
WISHING-START DOING* bump against the
pendant lights. Someone's cologne smells like floor
cleaner. We trace our feet on paper for a big-box
client and are gifted custom-fit shoes, smart with
Italian stitching, Brazilian rubber, Spanish leather. We
rock our way toward another all-hands meeting.

Memento Mori

How do I teach my child living in a house of perigold and crystal, mirror ball spinning out of control? We speed into traffic. Cars dart like unfed rats. We drive to a place of worship. Dry grass pokes through a concrete lawn. The royal doors are a lusterless French roast brown. Our footsteps echo in the vestibule. We look for the familiar Christ, the Virgin, host of saints. A hall of framed canvases emits sounds of the roiling sea.

A sale is on in the church basement, hats, rings, clutches, collectable mascot erasers, all emblazoned with a signature face—a flat-haired child praying, searchlight eyes, tiny hands inside muffs like a kitten, mouth agog as if watching a puppet show. A cherub? A warning of the inevitability of death? The gallery is festooned with carvings, portrait busts, paintings of this infernal innocent face. What is more fathomable, this child or a coral snake?

A sign on the wall says, *Suffer us not to go amisse, but as a father, helpe and guide us.* I had hoped for guidance, a way to a clean heart. My daughter gapes at the merchandise. Everything diminutive, infantilized, like the keychains that hang from her backpack. She rubs her hands together like a money changer. It has come, the cheapening. We hear voices, the dribbling of a faucet.

In the nave children pray on icon stands. Two nearby are kissing. One proffers a daisy. One rides a yellow ducky. It's a potty. He's doing his business saying *a-h-h-h*. In the ceiling, tube lights surround the Holy Ghost Hole, some red, some white, most too dim to see by. The vestry is filled with debris and haunt. Quench our thirst with living water. Where is a Priest when you need one?

How I Walk

In memory
pebbles like coins
undergrowth was different
trees were towering friends
roots curled
turning history over
like flat earth

Funeraria

They sent my mother to her grave with no jewelry.
She didn't have much

    A cameo of her mother's face
    or maybe it's Venus de Milo
    on a brooch of Sardonica shell
    A gold plate purse ashtray
    shaped like a tiny fry pan
    with a paste emerald on top
    Her Depression-era wedding band
    diamond the size of a fingernail clipping.

They should have buried her with amulets and silver snakes
    but instead they burned her in her dandelion color nightgown
        and lay her ashes in a white cardboard box
            that my father held in his lap on the airplane
                like a cake.

Power Pole

I harassed a crow the other day
big one up there
testing me
cawed four times
I cawed four times
then five
I did five
then four with a quarter note
I did same
he sped up
three four five-and-a-half.

Then like an impatient
conversationalist
he cut me off
and flew away
toward Whole Foods.

They recognize human faces
wonder what he thought of mine
his head cocked
bulging gray eye
reflecting the sun
like a marble.

Emerging Disciplines

Plastic spaceman in my fingers
hands a sky dock
skin tucked, air reaching in.
I welcome god, cloud, any line of light
that I am part of
my mouth, my face
the thinking I need to motate
like a robot on a cable delivering holiday notes
to aunts and uncles in a circle watching me work.
I feel their approval
smell rosy perfume, tobacco, and coffee.
Storm windows, chipped paint keep the cold out
glad for coal back then.
A box on the wall held house keys
skeleton keys capable of locking
in or out depending on my mood.
I throw my arms around the young child
all these years my nonsense lyrics
that make me laugh are derisive, mocking
the skein through which I taste me
amuse me, chastise me, wear my ribbons
like a desert operative.
I click on sales videos like looking in store windows
the threat, the truth, the real deal
why your liver worn on your head doth not a crown make
how to unearth you, contain you, sell you
for 99-fine gold, how to clean your clock,
dye your socks, end the shrieking
from neighbor to your elected official.
I have a few good habits
mat on the floor, long ribbed sandbag
a canvas yardstick, a smart spine,
a rubber occipital rest like two red handballs.
My daughter told me the more time
we spend flat on our backs the better.
Forgive, nay, adore the shimmering flesh.

Visit to the Bank

In a hallway of spotted granite, Mozart plays.
A host in satin lapels, chest framed like a moon
escorts me to an office with warm pink lamplight.

Behind a desk a banker sits
cocked like a palm tree
pick-axe cheeks, Picasso mouth.

Objects on his desk are stacked like underthings—
family photo of a boy in a t-shirt which reads
Money is my mood.

A plaque: *In spite of everything I still believe
that people are really good at heart.*
    —Anne Frank

Sober as dawn he says, *Whatever hurts in your life
we'll drown it in cash.* He is a hawk on rock,
eyes blank, the intimacy of his voice.

*You and I could clean up this city
brick by bullet hole.*
He hands me a glossy brochure.

In today's world water is rising, he says, *suicide is popular,
dogwalkers eat well. Upon your demise your house
will go to the bank like a Ferris wheel goes around.*

He turns his computer screen toward me
nodding his head for my virtual signature.
I sign with a flourish. I don't want to argue.

He is the picture of fathers.

View from Here

Tools essential to my life:
    The bitch
The gripe
    The whine

A box of silly fears
     Bag of automatic thoughts
        (she's tired of me,
               sexual prowess wanes,
                   I stink of demons)

I'm building a birdhouse for phobias
     with a perch for imaginary conflicts.
I'm determined to stop jutting my face out
     like a jack-in-the-box.
I lay fingers over my eyes to see the shadows
       rotate my thorax
rooted by the pelvis, an ancient children's dance
       thoughts like clouds,
feet on the floor. I wasn't surprised to learn
      from genomics
that I am descended from a bubble of intestinal gas
    from a seventeenth-century
Commedia dell'arte player, Pantalone in a royal
      Florentine family farce.

I come from solid stock
      sometimes liquid
     occasionally fire
        mostly earth.

In museums I've looked at squares of graphite swirls
    as though I were sifting light.

Given the chance to stare long and silent enough

at the bigger view—
   a hill of spruce
      a lightning strike
         rattling temblor

I am tapped by old sadness—little blue theater.
   I clear my mind
      like resetting a page

        churchy work.

Unconsecrated in Perugia

On the steps of the holy cathedral a security guard raises his arm
E chiuso. Non e consecrato, mi dispiace.
A decree has been penned, he says.
The Church of San Francesco al Prato has been unconsecrated—
now a godless vault stripped of adornments, absent of chalice,
liborium, and threads from the cassock of Saint Francesco.
For now souls will idle unprotected here.

In the nave below the altar
alongside the funerary monument of Geminiano Inghirami
rests a granite gray 715 horsepower V-12 Ferrari *Purosangue*
which now occupies the chapel just long enough
for this eight-speed dual-clutch Italian masterwork
to be made immortal in a TV commercial.

The axis of the church forms the cross, the shape of a human—
the narthex the foot, apse the head.
The shadow of a priest flutters through in a liturgical Roman cape
clutching his mitre. The stage crew adjusts lights,
car executives weigh costs, photographers charge their batteries.

Devotees are drawn to this stone-built shrine in spiritual pursuit
and prayer. The *Purosangue* with its prancing horse badge
and signature red-painted valves
does zero to sixty in 3.2 seconds.

As the moon rises, the west door is locked,
seminarians and novitiates creep
across the marble floor in ankle-length robes
secreting flagons of black plum.

One by one they run their fingers along its chrome
stroke its leather haunches, mount the luminous four-seater
and commence a bestial, boxerless romp,
hairless caresses, skin sliding, damask shredding

sex, drugs, and rock & roll black mass.

As the next day dawns the decree expires.
Purosangue is summoned to its car hauler.
Relics, crucifix and sanctuary lamp
are returned to their places.
Celebrants glide across the tabernacle
darkened in spirit and pray for mercy.

Cavern

We are lived by powers we pretend to understand.
—W.H. Auden

The firewall has collapsed between dream   fantasy   wish   hate
                a sizeless echo chamber of faces   memory,
                        nudes   trance dancers
                                measuring of time.

            I lay out my lunch on a white tablecloth
    little bowls   serrated knife   vitamins   bits of food wrap.
        So much to do.
                Must talk to the Centurion in my dream.

I interview a recurring bogeyman

Why are you here?

He says, *First your mother, then your dog, then your brother.*
You're next, it's your fate.

It's not my fate, I tell him. *I am a survivor.*

He fades out.

If I'd been sitting at a desk
I'd have continued the dialogue
I plan to query assorted selves in memory
welcome them in, be curious
I am not a foe.

I am relieved that the experts
admit to a lack of clarity on this process
even though philosophers sound so damned smart.

I'm hooked on memory   action pictures   vengeance

I grip my chair   gulp down popcorn   peel off into the street
                the fast bleed of wheels   gunfire
                        shouts and kisses.

I cast actors at every thought
they don't necessarily do what I want
just what my psyche puts out
actors often demur when you ask about technique.

Grief into Air

Occultist Massimiliano Palombara
bows deeply to his god.

A morel mushroom blooms by a tree stump
with children like thumbtack heads.

The old cypress across the way
practices the tarantella.

Clouds skate across the sun
leaving lakes of flour.

Chemistry seems to have failed
yet pots of sulphur continue to sluice

through the air night after night.
Horsehair strains his dreams of gold,

the stone spirit of his dead child,
a copper spoon, the love of his forebears.

The air bitter like his garden,
the water poisoned with mercury.

Blind to his madness, a splash of tea,
a piece of toast, the desire to boil.

Party

A towering red brick colonial
somewhat out of place
in the L.A. Basin which is a desert
serves small foods and rainbow drinks.
On the apron of the lawn balanced
on assigned squares of concrete
photographers cram together like pressed ham.
Some think they know me. They don't.
The blond host, gray Germanic eyes,
a bit of Howdy Doody to the ears, pulls at a bottle
of expensive syrup water like a hummingbird.
Eurotrash music drones from speakers on the walls.
A thin, braceleted woman in scuffed oxfords
sits askance, chewing gum, profile like a pistol.
I ask *Are you related or just a friend?*
She sinks into an adjoining room
where an antiques dealer holds forth
on romance and friendship,
My wife left me for a barn
stuffed with old armoires, he says.
Someone jokes about passing a hat.
All the names have left, one says.
I whisper my name just to hear it.
I taste toxins in the sparkling punch.
The room starts to spin like a space probe.
I begin to talk in an operatic baritone,
speaking on the mammalian brain,
our yen for violent sports, arbitrage.
Barn animal sounds come out of my mouth.
I look around the room.
The young seem bored.
The room is silent
but for the washing sound in my head.
Soon I will be at home.
I will sort this all out

in much the same way
as I arrange my sock drawer.

The Aristocrat

A nervous hold on power, nose like a parsnip
he sniffs pecorino for its age, horses for their gums.
A guywire from his mouth to God's ear he sucks
his long finger, pale hands big as dinner plates.

He dotes on his forebears in frescos, busts, oils,
family traits of Viking hair, tiny marble penises.
Blood is thicker than peasantry. Cousin Landolfo
is described in The Decameron as a pirate.

The aristocrat wears a tapering crown, arched brim,
a Beefeater bonnet to hide a congenital smirk
as if the right twist of cloth will keep his blood
blue and get him to heaven.

His craft is in the hand, the curve of the wrist,
outstretched arm, a bouquet of fingers pointing heavenward,
this is how Balanchine found his poses.
His weapon of choice a canon, royal as war can be.

Must be where the idea came for launching
servants over the lions' cage.
In the family chapel behind the presbytery is hidden
an ampoule of blood said to liquefy each year

on the anniversary of the martyrdom of St. Pantaleone,
a branch on the family tree of *Pantalone*,
a cunning and rapacious *Commedia* merchant
served by golden boys looted from a dusty past.

The aristocrat survives in a mute, crowded elegance
his privileged children like perfume bottles.
The family crest—a lion with a doubtful look
eating the head of a naked child.

Phone Power

I toss zipper bags and stand-up pouches
into a bucket and bring them
to the one place I know with a barrel
that says *Recycle Plastic Bags Here.*

I trudge through the parking lot muttering
Save the fish, save the fish.
My daughter calls it *wish-cycling.* Latest news
on plastic makers— like tobacco kings and big pharma—
they've made stuff up.

Your take-out box is not made from dinosaur skin
re-purposed to fling into a landfill to morph
to innocent crust to be used once again
as a hairpiece, a bicycle seat, a school-pack of pastel chalk.

Halfway through Trump's four-year gaseous horror
I wondered, what can I do? Then I remembered
how I once survived—selling over the phone,
can of Bugler Tobacco and papers on the desk
flipping card after card, calling mark after mark.

I signed up at the nearest Democratic phonebank.
First man I called said, *What do you want
to talk with my wife for? We vote Republican.*

I vamped: *Had lunch with Donald Trump last week,
and the guy really is a self-aggrandizing turd.*
(click)...I basked in the silence on the line.

I heard a celeb on TV say, *I hate the phone.*
What's to hate? It's a way in.

The Cartography of Knowing

A nurse gently hands me a wide digital plastic gray reader with buttons—where the buttons end and the edge begins. How novel. I was reading about this. A studio for my head, a conglomerate of mirrors, of continents, of museums I haven't visited and may never.

A nurse is on the phone. I can see her hair, it's brown in all the nice ways. She says the names of my wife and of my father—my father who has been gone nearly two-thirds of a century in medieval time.

I acknowledge her knowing of them. *Oh*, she says gravely, *you'd better come down*.

Now that I have a reader with plastic gray buttons intuition works as instruction. I'll go the way I often drift alone, across walks and streets, sitting on a sled of air, hardly using anything to stay afloat, like a Calcutta fakir rises from his cushion, like in the cartoons of all-knowing fools.

In an elevator a cube full of people nod their chins, knowing and not knowing each others' thoughts of needing cabbage for coleslaw, gas for carpool, refills of mood stabilizers and berberine.

If I know my dreams now, where's the excitement? Put back the scrim, the diamond-dotted sheer, the drop, the flat, the wall. Don't want an implant, don't want help from mad nuclear science practiced by robots. I'd rather wonder. *What do people really know? What did I know before these things happened?* What I do know is I want to wake up.

Thrusting into Reverence

A robot leans into the headwind like a hood ornament,
floats over the nearby schoolhouse, lands on my garden shed,
and disappears. I stand quietly so it will seem
like I am waiting for someone.

I pry open the door flaking splinters and wood rot.
Neat as an obsessive's laboratory, tools oiled, bandsaw
at the ready, titanium heads, eyes, arms, stacked
in corners, a dungeon of metallurgy.

Noises begin, a tin factory at dawn, wrenches click,
a rolling storage tote opens, and out flies a cartload
of gas monkeys who rip apart boxes of brand new
sleeveless jean jackets with gang insignia
on the back, god signs, wear them to the dance.

They climb on each other's backs, butts out like spare men,
voices all atremble. They flash finger signs, have hoses on,
camo gear, killer guns, ready for competition, programmed
to be no less intelligent than chats about sports betting.
A sign on the wall says: *If we can see God, we can be God.*

A tiny man sits at a work bench, bumpy head, a globe of flesh.
He squeezes his eyes shut. As if on the cover of Scientific American
robots appear at his side like knights on a chessboard—
new gods, hooded, gleaming, roosting,
big dreams, planted like duckweed.

Breathing the Space

Chicago Union Station just west of the river
between Adams and Jackson

a janitor walks her part of the evening
separate from the dwindling crowds.

How high the flatness
of the space in the fog of light.

She hears soft quaking
as the last passengers exit

the smell of purses
blossoming open.

The iron support beams
appear almost human.

She does not
reconstruct the past

or imagine the future;
she knows the instant now.

Slab floors and walls relax
like a massive marble sweater.

She chooses a portion to clean
viewing the space

in relation to the hours she must fill,
moving the detritus of a population

and sweeps it from behind
after they have gone—

what is removable
what is left.

America Made of Nails

An organized garage a whole-house idea
nothing small here forests of red cedar

the smell of dead trees
deserts of stumps the newness

big box dollies prefab panels clack bang
exquisite promise from the ground up

determined as an impatient parent
shelving dyed to resemble parkland

the promise of green.
where to chain a dog.

America is steel core sturdy next-level lean,
memories of the yard, expired smiles

hope for year-long vegetation
Jack at the fair with a handful of seeds

gardens of succulents grow through wars
storing moisture in neat rows of finished stalks

pots come in white cathedral
a plush black velvet ant hangs in the air

a carpenter bee works its wings in a weathered blossom
bores holes in a bare windowsill for its eggs.

We are low on water.
We require full sun to live.

Living with Ghosts

I felt guilty wanting a cheeseburger.
YMCA camp discouraged wanting
unless you wanted to witness
the divine power of nature manifested
in the whiff of lilacs, silvery flecks of waves on the lake
lines of bubbles on the surface of the water
made by giant white sturgeon fish.

Our counselor Jerry told a story in which
our skins dangle from sturgeons'
jaws in water where we swam.
I wanted a cheeseburger on a glossy brown bun—
earthly flesh, not heavenly flesh.
Memory of wanting is not memory of having
it is memory of seeing.

Staring ahead at the bowman's butt-crack
I hefted my paddle and paddled and paddled.
Lake Itaska was as big as the Sea of Galilee
I was bored by the relentless blue of the sky.
The clouds, Jerry explained, had been carted away
for cleaning, probably by God. Everything
was overseen by God. Except for ghosts.

Kirk, the kid I was stuck with in my canoe,
believed in ghosts. He tried to scare me
with his stories like a trick'or'treater thrusts
his pelvis into yours and demands more candy.
Kirk told a story about chisels hidden
in a hayloft where you swing on the barn rope,
drop into the hay, and are sliced in half.

After vespers Jerry told us ghost stories.
Kirk's stories were scarier and sadder. Maybe Kirk
was on the camp payroll, forcing us closer to God,

making us take comfort in the nightly recitation:
Watch and guard me through the night
Jerry said aloud with us, before the braying of the ghosts.

Darkness

His hand on my shoulder Scott and I
head toward the airline check-in counter.
His hip grazes a luggage cart.

I've been losing my sight for 30 years, he says.
Waiting for the wheelchair attendant
I'm not so much starting to miss Scott

as thinking about the darkness that envelops him.
He tells me about riding alone on a bus
still able to see shapes and forms

sometimes facial expressions.
On the bus a man across the aisle stares.
Poor guy, he says. *He can't see, he can't see.*

He comes over, sits down,
puts his hand on Scott's cheek,
and slaps him.

You're okay, you're okay,
the man says
before he gets off the bus.

Don't Waste Time

Your stringy little dog all blonde
your dish detergent Dawn
how it blues the sun

I imagine palmfuls of thick, pliant dirt
under your roses behind a cedar fence
an impressive harvest

let's connect privately
safe for all
we have several options

we can discuss
generic loss
pet bird, plush toy

we could say nervous words
crummy tie   pee fight   throw chop chop
or search for people who

have undergone similar experiences
I don't fear an English kiss
your skin for good effect

we'll play off each other
I sometimes play catch
but mostly I just sit here

I should do more
I reached out once
through a marriage monger's office

I watched a person from behind
in a viewing booth
eject my video

I never returned
my triggers include the wreck of loneliness
chainlink too much blush

I'm not anchored in place
look at my words separately
message back

If Everything Turns Out as Hoped

I'll be in silks and tweeds, feet light as facial
puffs
    shoes long as a breadbox, snapshots of every
    pair
        framed in a neatly edited grid
      on my kitchen wall by the frypans.

Complete control like a good camp counsellor
  all moods swinging like hammocks
    drug damage no longer damage
      smiling memories of fatuous youth.

Buddhist chants—wishful ones, loving kindness
ones—
    will come true
    war no more please war no more.

No suspicions: *Look at that nose, I wonder if he...*

Life, a farm of pages suited for baking.
    Nightly screenings of Jung Freud Marx
      Bishop Baldwin Plath

you won't need a pass you are already registered.

Poems, stories, philosophical truths
    gathered like flocks of pigeons ready to feed
      psychic powers I turn on
        like indirect lighting in elevators.
          I'll edit my thoughts so strangers
            keep their good image of me.

No fears that anyone is not watching,
    relieved that family, teachers, dogs
      all watched enough, so I can rest.

It'll all be enough, plentiful like wheat, like the
stars.
Humans will achieve newness
    conversations will flow like waterfalls
       people will sparkle like much-loved
          cartoons.

If It Wasn't for You

I'd be a baby without skin, a parrot
without a soap-shaped food cake,
a truck driver out of a job,
I used to envy those guys
name on the side, tools in the back.

If it wasn't for you I'd be bread, old, stale,
baked out, dirt under a mat, a neon sign
that isn't pretty. I'd be the smell of rot after a rain,
the hostility of the locker room, the sting of the pool.

I'd be a pool cue wrapped around a stranger's head.
I'd be dead or at least without significance.
I'd be a salad without dressing I'd be a bug
with no special genus untraceable alone.

Sitting on an island I'd be corn in teeth,
shit on mushrooms, nylon on Saran Wrap,
string between lovers, teen angels,
old '78s I could spin out the window

and crack against the neighbor's clapboards.
I'd be memories without sense as in a dream
driven by dialogue, sentences that make sense
in class but of no context, adding things up

tearing things out as if they were coupons,
dry, bald, seated, in only mild pain.
Is this what you expected?
Don't answer until I'm out of the room.

Our Losses Return to Us

Long after other dreams
my mother comes back

like an ancient celebrity in a hotel
with an appointment secretary

Before you see her you need to know
she is in a very fragile state, says the man

I am no longer trusted
walled off by protocol

her papery skin, dry viscera
decades under the sod at Saint James Kingsessing

I need to tell her
how hard it was to do without her

Perhaps I am being unfair
a bit too needful

Promptly the dream slides away
like lamb from a meat slicer

Acknowledgments

Thanks to the editors below who have published the following poems:

"Delores" *Love in the Original Language,* Moonstone Press Anthology
"Empathy" *Poems For All*
"Full Wolf Moon" *Gyroscope Review*
"If It Wasn't For You" *Lascaux Review*
"Memento Mori" *Sledgehammer*
"My Brother is a Dark Circus" *Book of Matches*
"Party" *I-70 Review*
"That Your Heart Longs For" *Abandoned Mine*
"They Send Me to the City to Stay with My Auntie" *Gyroscope Review*
"Things at Work That Pass for Art" *The Courtship of Winds*
"Thrusting Into Reverence" *Science Fiction Poetry Association Halloween 2023*
"Funeraria" *Tiny Moments: Vol. V* Bronze Bird Books

Thanks ⌐

to the poets & writers who have taught me to write:

Jack Grapes, Alexis Rhone Fancher, Jill Alexander Essbaum, Peggy Dobreer, Kim Addonizio, Carol Frost, Craig Cotter, Terry Wolverton, Kim Dower, Don Kingfisher Campbell, G.T. Foster, Perie Longo, Elya Braden, Jon Pearson, Art Hanlon, Jacinta White, Kelly Grace Thomas, Tresha Faye Haefner, Mehnaz Sahibzada, Armine Iknadossian, Mary Wood, Nancy Scherlong, Richard Blanco, Richard Jones, Jennifer Clement, James Fenton, Rachel Kann, Luis Alberto Urrea, Brendan Constantine, and Donna Baier-Stein.

Bill Ratner

is a voice actor and author of the poetry collection *Fear of Fish* (Alien Buddha Press 2021,) poetry chapbook *To Decorate a Casket* (Finishing Line Press 2021,) *Parenting For The Digital Age: The Truth Behind Media's Effect On Children And What To Do About It* (Familius Books 2014,) and a Best of the Net Poetry Nominee 2023 (Lascaux Review.) His writing appears in Best Small Fictions 2021 (Sonder Press,) Missouri Review (audio,) anthology *Sh!t Men Say to Me* (Moon Tide Press,) Baltimore Review, Chiron Review, Feminine Collective, and other journals. He is a 9-time winner of the Moth StorySLAM, an officer in his union SAG-AFTRA, a trained grief counsellor, and teaches Voiceovers for SAG-AFTRA Foundation and Media Awareness for Los Angeles Unified School District. billratner.com/author • @billratner

Slow Lightning Lit Titles

Lamenting While Doing Laps in the Lake,

Bill Ratner 2024

*

Living Poetry

Murray Mednick 2024

*

As Man Is to God: A Poem

on the Making of Werner Herzog's "Fitzcarraldo"

By Andrew Nicholls 2024

*

Slow Lightning III: Folio Edition 2025

Slow Lightning II: Astonished Poetry 2024

Slow Lightning I: Impractical Poetry 2022

www.slowlightninglit.com

Made in the USA
Columbia, SC
28 November 2024

47332117R00052